AS STILL AS WATER

TEN THINGS THAT TEN PHOTOGRAPHS TAUGHT ME

RAJAT SEBASTIAN

XpressPublishing
An imprint of Notion Press

XpressPublishing
An imprint of Notion Press

No.8, 3rd Cross Street,CIT Colony,
Mylapore, Chennai, Tamil Nadu-600004

ISBN 978-1-63633-977-1

"Empty your mind, be formless, shapeless, like water.

If you put water into a cup, it becomes the cup.

You put water into a bottle and it becomes the bottle.

You put it in a teapot it becomes the teapot.

Now, water can flow or it can crash.

Be water, my friend."

- Bruce Lee

Contents

"Don't think about making art, just get it done. Let everyone else decide if it's good or bad, whether they love it or hate it. While they're deciding, make even more art."
- Andy Warhol

To all the photographers out there - Don't take a photograph.
Make it.

About The Author

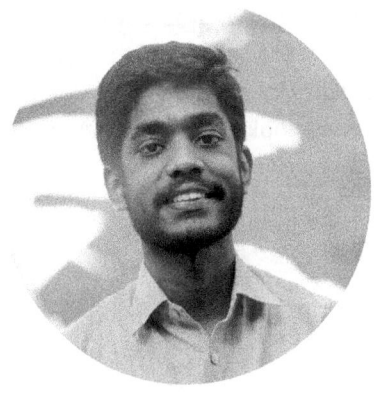

Rajat Sebastian

A research scholar and freelance photographer, Rajat Sebastian is a native of Kochi, Kerala and is currently pursuing his PhD in English Studies from CHRIST (Deemed to be University), Bangalore. Starting with landscape photography as a hobby in 2016, he now helps people see the beauty in almost everything.

After completing his schooling from Kendriya Vidyalaya NAD Aluva, Rajat completed his Bachelor of Arts degree from De Paul Institute of Science & Technology, Angamaly in English Literature, Communication and

Journalism. He went ahead to complete post-graduation in MA English with Cultural Studies from CHRIST (Deemed to be University), Bangalore.

Most of the time, Rajat shares his works on his website and Instagram focusing on wildlife, landscape, nature and creative photography. Part of the story is an image and he believes in the power of photography as a medium that can tell stories which words often fail to describe.

Website:*www.rajatsebastian.com*

Instgram, Facebook and Twitter:*@rajatsebastian*

Prologue

Art always amazed me and helped improve myself. I scored good marks in science in my school but never after class X. It was only later in my life that I understood everything is art – from what we say to what we do. Art takes many forms to express itself, from painting to music to dance and much more. It is said that there is an art in science too. I chose photography as a medium to share the art I see and feel in this world, not because I am an expert in photography, but because of its ability to freeze time. I always feel happy when I see people like you coming up with unique, beautiful photographs that hold my mind still – as still as water. It has been only three years since I took up this passion and converted it into a hobby when a lot of things started confusing me like how they confuse you now. I didn't know when to make my photographs black and white and which camera to choose. I didn't know if I should select a genre of photography to specialise and what makes a picture look good. I started searching answers for these questions only to get confused by several more. Later I realised that the answers were always there in the photographs I took. I then relooked ten pictures I took over these three years, recalled when and how I captured them, what lessons they taught me and is finally sharing them here. Those lessons are the chapters in this book. It is not only the way I captured these images that teach us something but also the story behind those frames.

I am sure that most of you will be able to relate to what I say but may also differ in some ideas. Ultimately, these are all my viewpoints, and I wish to know what readers like you have to say. As art is something as infinite as a human mind, the questions that pertain to photography are also the same. I have considered only ten of my works not only because they are my personal favourites but also because they answer the most common questions. I hope I could put my heart out, remove your doubts and fill you with confidence through this work. Together, let us freeze time and decorate this world with our art.

1

Believe

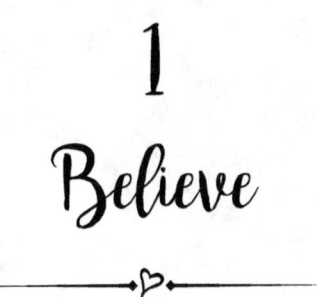

"Seeing is not believing. It's the other way round. Believe, and you will see."
– El Orfanato (2007) by Juan Antonio

ᗞᗞᗞ

It was around the last few days of August this year. Kerala was expecting the third flood, with people struggling to find safe shelters amidst a pandemic. I live in a small village called Kunnukara, somewhat near to Manjaly known for its Biriyani and Halwa. The weather was cloudy as usual with red alerts issued to more than five districts at the same time. My neighbours, relatives and friends moved to safer locations as Kuttipuzha was just one kilometre from river Periyar. Periyar had flooded Kuttipuzha once in 2018 as the river flow through many Dams in Kerala.

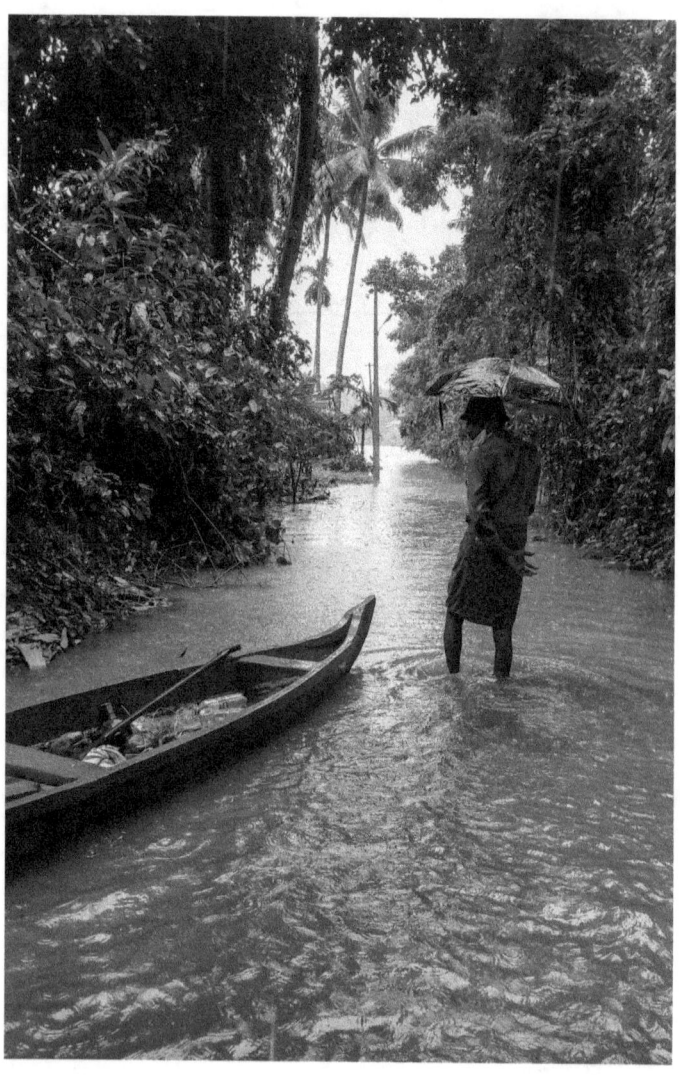

My family had planned to move within three days if the situation got worse. When the continuous downpour came to a halt, I decided to take a walk with my dad through my deserted village and have a look at the river. We expected the water level to be alarmingly high, but the condition was worse. The water was at the level of our knees even when the river was half a kilometre away. Taking risks, we both decided to continue walking until it felt as if a further movement was impossible. Torrent of water flowed against us. We were about to turn back when we noticed a man standing still, facing the river. He was not moving but was drowned in his thoughts – maybe the thought of losing his belongings. We thought he may need some help and struggled to reach near him who was not even making a move. A traditional boat lay beside him, tied to an electric post. It contained some dress, food and drinking water enough for one man to strive for the next seven days. On further enquiry, we realised that we never knew who that man was. He had settled in our village a week ago, earned 250 square feet of land near the river and built there a tent to live. The previous week was spent entirely on farming which was now underwater.

"Why are you waiting here, Cheta?" my dad asked.

He did not reply.

"Cheta?" Dad called again.

"I should not have done this." He said.

"But you did not expect a flood this time. Nobody did. Why should we not do anything just because we are afraid?" I asked.

The banana saplings lay submerged as if calling for help.

"It's not the farm. It's what I did to nature. I should have left alone some space for the river, but I didn't. The river is now claiming back what belongs to her".

The man was not crying because he had lost his land or his work went in vain. He was not sad because he did not have anywhere else to go, but because he regretted his action of compromising nature for his benefits. I immediately recalled a quote I read that day - "It's just one plastic straw, said seven billion people".

Most of the time, we never care what the story behind a picture is. We just check who captured the photograph and whether it pleases our eyes. I never cared about what device I had with me and what settings I shot with. All that I had in my mind was to show the world what this one human being was doing – regretting his action of compromising nature. Pictures cannot actually speak but can make you feel as if they do. Look for the story, emotion or beauty and let the camera do its work. Let's concentrate on that part whether the photograph you took can speak or not. There are stories everywhere. Nature has a story to tell. Even the animals, birds and insects out there are looking for you to tell their stories. If you have a camera that can paint thousands of tales with one picture, that is enough to make it a photograph.

So, how do you grab stories to click? The first thing I would like to say is that never search for a tale just because you want to capture something. Never capture a random photo and attribute random stories. Observe your surroundings, go to the nearby street for a walk and visit the garden or the park. You will find that almost everything around us has something to say. It can be people engaged with something, animals greeting each other or even the nature trying to express itself. When you start observing and understanding, you will realise how easy it is to find a story so that you can capture and turn it into a photograph.

Water was rushing in; we couldn't stay long at that place where we met that man. We asked him to come with us, but he didn't, saying he will be there for a little longer. He has the traditional boat by his side for escape. Going back, I turned to look at that man once again - still standing like a statue. I took my phone and clicked a picture. My camera was in B&W mode and not in proper settings, but at least I got a photograph to keep and cherish for a lifetime. At least I have a picture that speaks.

I uploaded the photo to my drive.

2

Wonder

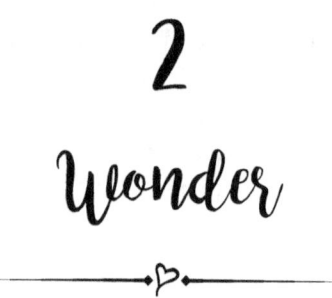

"The two most powerful warriors are patience and time."
- Leo Tolstoy

🍥🍥🍥

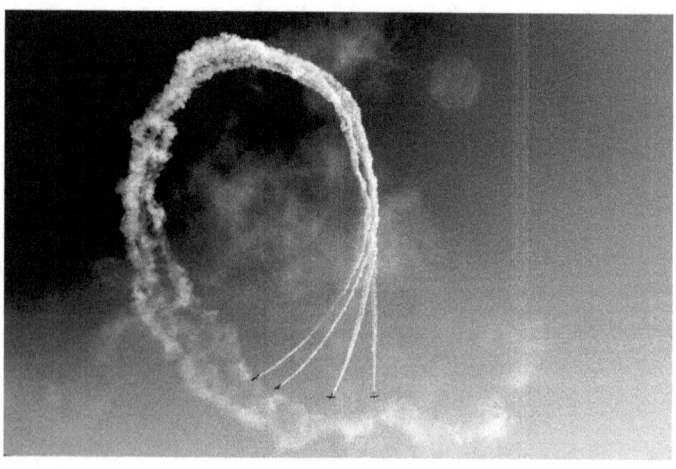

It was already ten minutes past seven in the morning when I left my hostel to Yelahanka. Taking an autorickshaw to Yelechenahalli metro station, I was flying in the three-coach metro train to Majestic. I planned to catch an airport bus to get down at Yelahanka bus stop where the famous Aero India show was happening. Walking through Kempegowda bus depot, I wondered why there were more buses at the terminal allocated for airport buses when I heard people shouting "Air Show".

To my surprise, Bangalore Metropolitan Transport Corporation had already arranged numerous special buses for Aero India which they lovingly called "Air Show". While it was 40 rupees per head in a non-A/c bus, it was around 90 per head in an A/c one. I boarded a non -A/c bus thinking of saving money. Unfortunately, it was the A/c buses that made its destination earlier. A long struggle of one hour in traffic jams and scorching heat got me to Yelahanka bus stop only to find one had to walk three km to the Air Force Base station. We all started walking as there was no auto-rickshaw or cab available. The show began at sharp 10 AM, while we reached by 10:20 AM. We rushed to the venue only to find another long queue to verify online tickets. Anyhow, standing there, one could watch the fighter planes rolling in the sky.

Amidst all the chaos that occurs in a queue full of people, I took out my camera without even caring what lens I had on it. Whenever I tried to click a picture, either the person behind will push me, or the one in front will move forward to make some progress in the queue. Anyhow, I couldn't click one single photograph properly. I finally decided to stop multitasking as I understood that standing there and photographing aeroplanes at the same time is not a good idea. The queue seemed to be moving in a quick phase until I almost reached its end. Someone in the front seemed to have something prohibited in his bag, probably food items.

The queue got stuck. People yelled. I thought it as a chance to test my photography skills again and took out my camera once more. Three fighter planes had taken off by that time, and I imagined them to be my object for capture. I still don't know what models of aeroplanes were they, but I guess the pilots were instructed to do some summersaults. Summersault with three fighter planes are never easy as they must be taken to greater altitudes in the sky. I felt lucky at that point because all the people in the queue can now see that stunt standing there itself, without having to go to the gallery. I pointed my camera towards those three fighter planes that seemed to have defied the laws of physics. I never cared what mode my camera was in but clicked what I saw in front of my eyes. If I took one second more to adjust the camera settings, neither would have I been able to see what I saw nor would have I been able to capture it. From that time, I realised what the word timing meant and why I should never comprise such an integral factor with settings. In the end, it is the photograph that matters but not the camera settings with which you shot it.

Further on, security personnel verified my ticket and asked me to rush if I was a photographer. Maybe he saw the DSLR camera I kept back in my bag. The venue was an open ground separated with huge barricades. While the public had to stand on one side, fighter planes and helicopters took off from the other. There were already hundreds enjoying the show like photographers with gears I had seen only in photography magazines. Almost all the pilots greeted the audience before take off, waving their hand towards us. Once they were in the sky, they seemed to defy gravity, fear and the laws of physics. Some stunts seemed impossible that they blocked my breath and I couldn't capture them but just keep watching. Amidst all the applause and appreciations, I wondered what the pilots felt sitting inside those aircraft upsides down. Each performance lasted around ten minutes. It was a moment of pride for the country and those pilots who were willing to risk their lives to make their country and countrymen proud. Even the sky was full of wonder, seeing the performance under!

3

Conspire

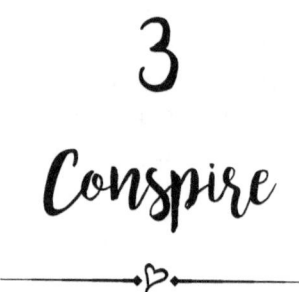

"When you want something, all the universe conspires in helping you achieve it."
– Paulo Coelho

ᗡᗡᗡ

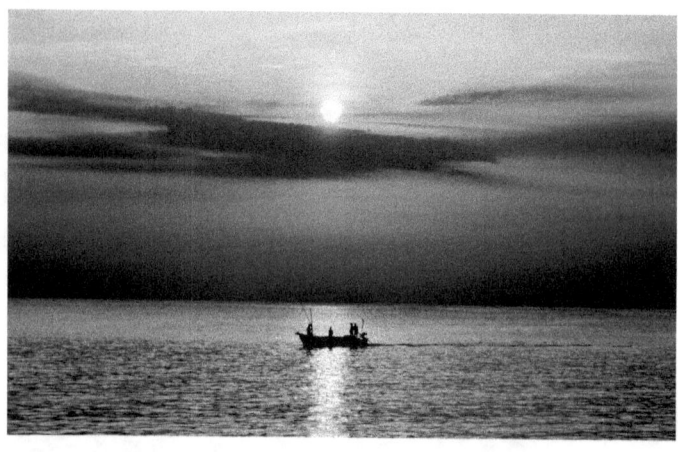

Calm day. Peaceful vibes. The sun and fishermen rose as usual. Reaching the horizon on time was a mission for both. At last, they did, but while the sun lit up the world, the fishermen were still busy searching for a catch.

It was around 5:30 in the morning when I left my hotel to see the sunrise from Kanyakumari. As it was my first time in that part of the country, I was late at the viewpoint. Though I rushed, I was not lucky as it was a cloudy day. The sunrise was still visible but not in its usual glory. There was no other option other than to enjoy what I had in front without being able to capture the kind of shots I had in my mind. The clouds never seemed to move from its place, and all I could do was to capture what I saw. Standing at the seashore clicking random pictures (with mostly clouds in the front and sun at the back), I also saw fishermen moving in groups searching for fish. Next moment, three fishermen who were in a traditional boat together went past the horizon as I waited for them to be in alignment with the rays of the sun. Surprisingly, on reaching that particular point at the sea where I exactly wanted them to be, they stopped for a minute and found a catch. I don't know how many times I pressed my shutter button, but it was this given image that I ultimately felt the best amongst them all.

Clouds added beauty to the image as the frame would not have been as perfect as it is if there were no clouds visible. The sun, clouds and fishermen aligned themselves over a calm sea just for one minute when I captured this image. There was no one there besides me as most of them left disappointed, unable to see another sunrise. I knew that there were a thousand images of the sunrise shot from Kanyakumari on the Internet. Still, photographs that included multiple aspects of that place were rare. Before I left that beautiful place on earth, I felt as if nature was talking to me – appreciating my patience and love for her. If you are someone who loves to freeze time, what more can I say to you than to be patient, take time, slow down and watch how the universe help you achieve what you desire?

Before going to my hotel room from the viewpoint, I saw three fishermen reach back ashore with the day's catch. I recalled how three fishermen paused at the horizon in perfect alignment with the sun, finding their prey at that exact point in that vast sea. Out of curiosity, I approached them to check whether they were the same people I captured in my frame. They were indeed the same people who stopped at a point where there was 'too much sunlight'. They didn't realise that they were in perfect alignment with the rising sun and that they were being photographed by me. The conversation that followed is unbelievable.

"We don't usually get any catch from that point, but today we did. We were wondering why", one said in half Tamil and half Malayalam.

"The nature is unpredictable Anna", said the second fisherman. "We never know how it reacts. Sometimes it surprises us, otherwise, disappoint. Maybe nature should remain that way itself. It's all some secrets", he said.

"That's the beauty of this universe", the third man completed the conversation.

4

Surprise

—◦♡◦—

"Let every frame that you capture should be one that you admired and not what you took to impress others."

♡♡♡

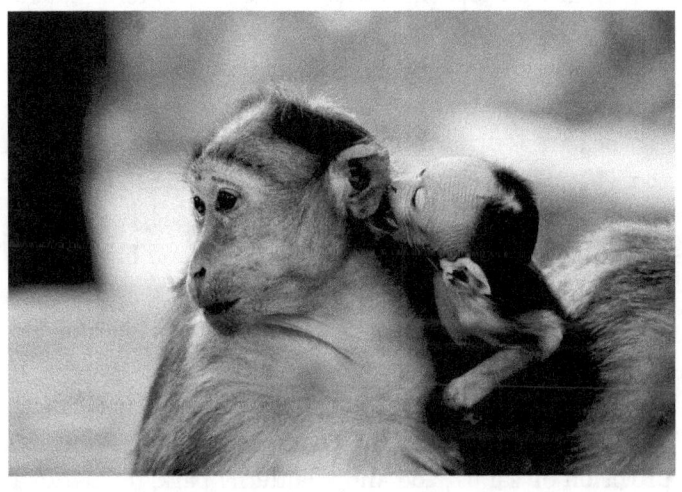

Often, things may not go as you planned but make sure you make the best out of what the world offers you. Whenever I imagine a frame and try to capture it with my camera, it often happens that I may not get the desired image. If it is not because of the way you imagined the frame to be or because of the settings of the camera, why worry when we cannot control the universe? All that we can do is to wait and make the best out of what we have in front because a picture is more than a thousand words. I would like to share one such experience through this story.

Bannerghatta in Bangalore is a place known for its National Park. More than a National Park, I think one can find a lot more in this village, which is now turning into a town. The Shiva temple on top of a hill is one such attraction along with places like Thottikallu waterfalls. For nearly seventeen months, I have seen buses with number 365 written on top. All those crowded buses terminate at Bannerghatta National Park, showing how important the place is. The park is usually crowded on Saturdays, Sundays and other public holidays.

The park is divided into two parts - open zoo and closed zoo. The open zoo let visitors take a tour inside an enclosure where animals are left free, and the closed zoo gives a traditional viewing experience – animals and birds inside cages. Ticket fare varies with visitor's needs, depending on whether you want to carry a camera, shoot videos or just take a 'safari' to the open zoo. The safari also comes in different packages and can be chosen between riding in an air-conditioned car or an eighteen-seater bus. With this provision of 'safari', zoo and a butterfly park, the national park also attracts tourists with the serenity of that place. I visited the park about five times during my two years of stay in Bangalore. They were mainly to accompany my

14

friends who came to Bangalore and wanted to go somewhere 'different'.

"Forget cafeterias, shopping malls and gardens, let's go somewhere different", they would say. The only options that come to my mind then are Bannerghatta National Park or Thottikallu waterfalls. It was during one such visit that I took my camera with me. I could click a couple of pictures inside the zoo but was not happy with any of them as the animals were confined to cages. I felt that their beauty can be seen only when they are free in their habitat. As I came out of the park still holding my camera, I saw a few monkeys playing beside the exit gate. They were, of course, free, hanging and jumping over the branches of a pine tree. Some of them occasionally came down to check whether humans would feed them.

In contrast, the others observed everything from the top of the tree. As there was a cafeteria near the exit gate, most of the visitors to the park spend some time there to can refresh themselves before leaving the place. Such people often buy snacks for monkeys and keep it under trees so that monkeys can eat them. My attention was caught by a plate of food that lay under a tree. A group of monkeys came to feed on it as I noticed the happiness they had on their face – of being free. Some babies were hanging on to their mother. I wished to take a shot of those monkeys to record that ultimate happiness of freedom planning to compare those images with that of the pictures of the monkeys put inside cages. I readied my camera and knelt to take some close-up shots when one baby monkey playfully tried to bite the ears of her mother. She was about to bite when I pressed the shutter of my camera, with the shot capturing another powerful emotion called love. It was one of the best one I could ever take. I never compared that picture with any other photos but just posted it with one caption - "You may outgrow her lap, but never her heart"!

5
Shades

—◦❦◦—

"When you photograph people in colour, you photograph their clothes. But when you photograph people in B&W, you photograph their souls."
– Ted Grant

❦ ❦ ❦

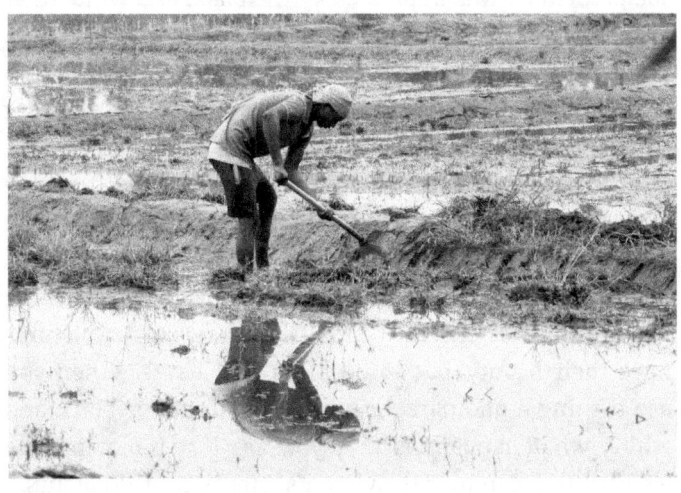

From the day I started spending time with nature, paddy fields were my favourite spots. Covered with water, mud and crops, I was always fascinated by the hard work of farmers who spend their day and night taking care of the rice crops in those paddy fields. Sometimes I could see leeches, frogs and even snakes. But as you know; nature works in perfect harmony with all these living beings required for its functioning.

On my birthday I went to the paddy fields in the morning as I had thought of attending the church that evening. As expected, there were farmers around the farm ploughing and sowing. While many were far away in that vast plots of land, my camera couldn't zoom much to capture everyone. Whenever one bent and stroked the plough, I noticed his reflection on the water in the field. I clicked a picture with the farmer above and his crystal-clear reflection below but got troubled when I tried to post it on a social media. I was impressed by the black and white filter offered by the site and felt that it added beauty to the image. The photograph was ultimately processed and posted as a black and white image when I started wondering why is it that the absence of colours added beauty to the picture.

It is always confusing whether or not we have to make a photo black and white to bring out some aesthetics. You might have clicked a beautiful picture in colour from a nearby street when you saw a street photographer posting his works in black and white. Of course, colour pictures have their beauty, but so do black and white. When you are turning a photograph into monochrome or black and white, what happens is that you are just removing one element that captures the viewer's attention – the colours.

Whenever you cry, pray and or feel joy, you may close your eyes so that you can feel what you are doing. Whenever you remove colours from a photograph, I think you will start feeling the emotions in it rather than viewing them. Some stories are better when experienced than seen. Of course, it is not that only black and white images contain emotions. On the other hand, they may be able to convey those emotions more intensely than pictures shot in colour.

If a picture does not have colour, the viewers will search for emotion conveyed or a story behind the frame. Thus, a black and white image is something that focuses on emotions narrated through the picture than on the visual pleasure it can give through its vibrant colours. Next time, when you are confused about whether to post a picture in black and white or colour, think what purpose your image is going to serve. Does it want the viewers to just see the beauty in your frame? Or does it want to convey a deep emotion? Then I guess you are good to go.

6

Sense

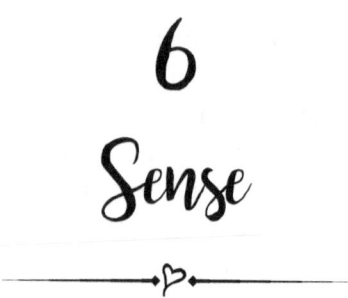

"If it makes you happy, it doesn't have to make sense to others."

🐾🐾🐾

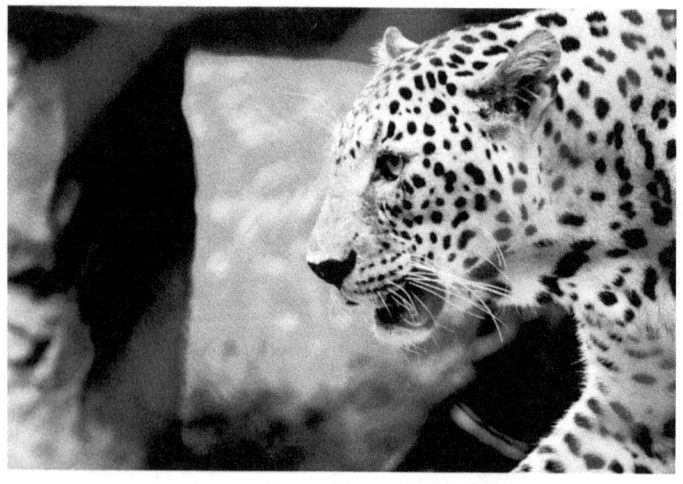

"A leopard in a cage? Is that ethical?" asked my friend when I showed him this picture. I didn't know what to answer, so I showed the same photograph to another friend. "I am sure you didn't click this one. Which website allowed you to download it?" she asked.

Most of the times, people cannot accept your growth or the fact that you are improving yourself. It was during the initial days of getting a camera that I got a chance to visit the zoo in Thiruvananthapuram, Kerala. Just like the name of the south Indian district, the park was also huge – with all the animals being caged. I knew it was not fair to do some wildlife photography with caged animals as they were not in their natural habitat. However, I considered the zoo as a place to practice wildlife photography so that I can use the skills attained later in real forests. From squirrels to parrots, I captured everything I could - testing different modes and settings of the camera when I reached the section where leopards, tigers and lions were caged. I clicked the pictures of tigers and lions laying on the ground, depressed, which made me delete those pictures then and there itself. It was then the turn to look at how the leopards were doing. I went near a cage where I saw the label 'Indian Leopard'. Surprisingly, the cell was quite big, with enough space for at least five leopards to roam around. I came to know that there was only one leopard inside that cage but was not visible. I saw some yellow spots moving at the other end. Assuming it to be the leopard, I kept my camera ready. I had no time to put on the zoom lens and hence decided to continue with the 'small lens' that can zoom only up to a maximum of five meters. Suddenly, the leopard jumped out from a nearby bunch of grass.

I was standing very close to the cage with my camera focused on the other end of the cell. The leopard couldn't touch me as the cage bars were covered with metallic net. Annoyed by the same, he started walking to the left side of the cage with me standing there shocked, and my camera focused on the other side of the cell. While the leopard was walking to the left, I pressed the shutter button when his face came inside the 3.2-inch display. Of course, I got a rare picture as if taken with a professional camera from a jungle, but the real problem was ethics. Neither can I lie that the photograph was captured in the forest, nor can I resist myself from sharing it with the world. At last, I remembered the story behind the picture. I recalled how the leopard jumped out of the bush and how his anger of not being able to catch me was shot into a photograph.

I can say three things with this photograph. First, most of the times, it's the story behind a picture that adds up its beauty. Second, always be true to yourself and the work you do, like how I shared the exact story behind this picture with you. Third, and most important, what you do doesn't need to make sense to others. It was only my decision to capture the photos of animals inside the zoo that helped me understand a lot of settings of my camera. My decision enabled me to practice wildlife photography in a controlled environment. People will have their opinions about everything – they may mock you for capturing a leopard's photo from a zoo than a forest. But ultimately, you will be benefitted, not only because you will get practice and knowledge but also unique pictures that carry emotions. After all, as Arch Hades said, your worth is not determined by someone's ability to appreciate it.

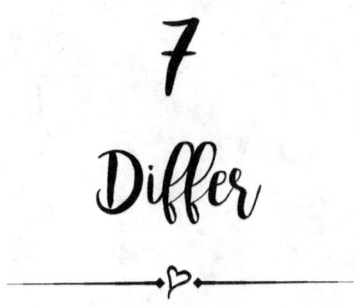

7
Differ

"Learn the rules like a pro so that you can break them like an artist."
– Pablo Picasso

 PPP

Picasso, as you know, never meant to break any laws or rules but to use artistic freedom of expression. When it comes to photography, you may capture beautiful, unique photographs and find out new ways of creating beautiful frames. Nowadays, there are many so-called 'tools' in the market that helps you make creative frames. One such tool is the lens-ball that converges the light falling on it to a point at its centre. We also have prisms that create triangular shaped frames. Anyhow, there is that one single question which arises when we use these tools – are they ethical? Shouldn't we capture frames as they are?

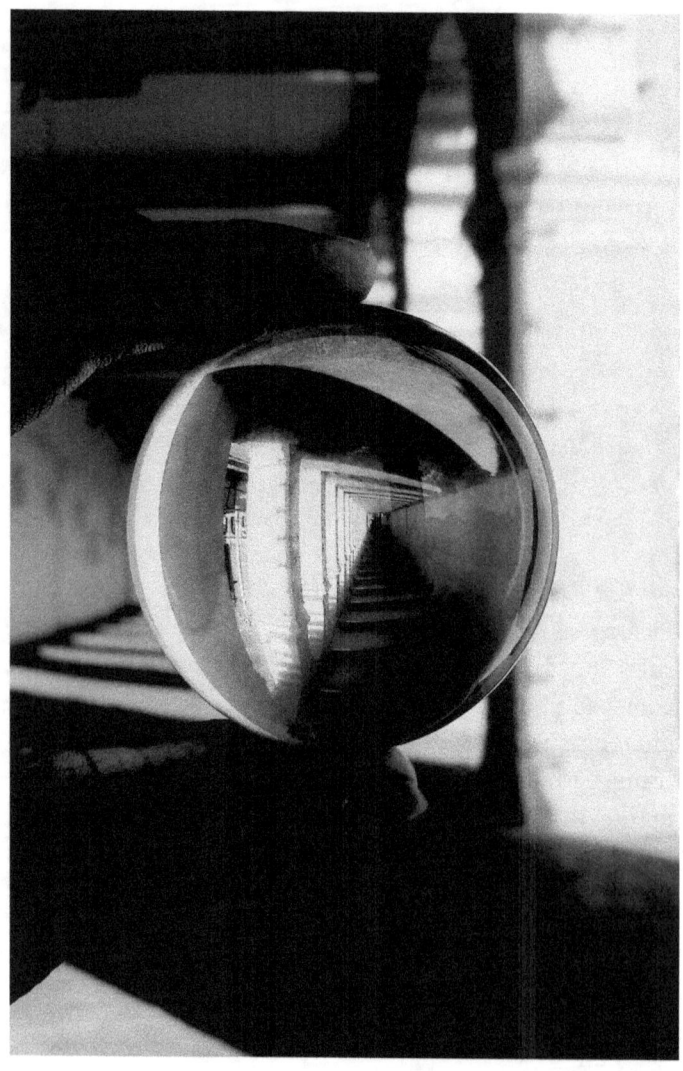

I also had this same doubt when I got a chance to visit Mysore Palace. Mysore is one of the most famous tourist destinations near Bangalore as both cities are just two hours apart if we travel by train. One day, on getting a day off from my college, I decided to visit the place with my friend and enjoy at least one spot there. We wanted to leave Bangalore by the train at 6:30 AM. After getting up late and stuck in the Bangalore traffic, we could depart only at 11 AM reaching Mysore by 1 PM. The spot which we chose to explore was none other than the Mysore Palace. It took us more than three hours to view the palace and was amazed by its architecture. Exiting the monument by four in the evening, we noticed that there were elephants at one corner of the palace ground taken care of by two people.

We wanted to observe them and click some pictures when we realised that it was a restricted area. Disappointed and tired, we were about to return when a small building nearby caught our attention. We figured out that it was an old annexure building of the palace but didn't know why was it built. The building had the same architectural style as of the Mysore Palace. It was closed for some maintenance work, and we were able to observe it only from outside. The veranda was built with a lot of pillars that stood as the central support for the building. It also created a particular pattern which I captured standing at one end of the veranda and pointing my camera to the other. Such shots of patterns in architecture are typical, and I didn't feel as if the picture I took was different. I needed something unique for which I decided to use my lens-ball. I stood at the same point and kept the lens-ball at my eye level to see how it made all the pillars of the building appear as if they emerged from the centre of that ball. I clicked the shutter button happily as I was able to capture a frame differently.

When you feel confused about whether you need to use any tool like a lens-ball that may manipulate the original view, think why you want to use that tool in the first place. Is it because you want a different frame? Or is it because the object in your frame becomes beautiful only when you use a tool like a lens-ball? One thing you have to remember is that using a tool like a lens-ball automatically classifies an image into the category of creative photography than any other genre. Hence, it will be better if you can answer those two questions before you use innovative tools next time. As always, the photograph you capture is ultimately your work of art, and you have the freedom to choose how that should be.

8
Work

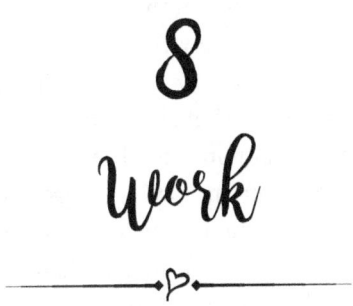

"If you cannot do great things, do small things in a great way."
– Napolean Hill

❧❧❧

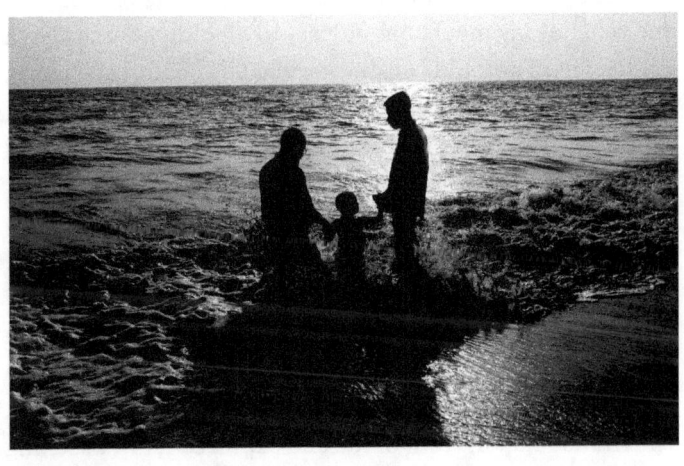

Two years before, I got a chance to present a paper at the Young Scholar's Congress, Thiruvananthapuram. I had a great time during the conference and could meet many people from different parts of the country. Day one got over by four in the evening, giving some time to relax and explore the city. I set out to Shangumugham beach near the Trivandrum International Airport. The beach was not as crowded as usual, but one could see children playing and local vendors and tourists having a great time. I walked around the beach for some time and stopped at a point to view the sunset. As it was getting dark, a lot of the people started leaving while I decided to stay a little longer. I was trying to click some pictures of the sunset when I noticed some families enjoying their time in the sea.

I heard a child being called back by his mother from the sea as he stood aside on the shore with a heavy heart. His feelings are relatable as we all might have gone through such moments at least once in our life. Suddenly, a man of the kid's dad's age came and held his hand. He took him to the sea, not far much, but at least to a point where the sea hit his feet. The child became very happy again and started enjoying the sea-waves holding the hands of that man. I wished to capture a photo of that particular scene and went to seek their permission.

As I was about to reach near them, I saw another man accompany those two. The third man who came and held the other hand of the child was an aged man who changed the entire scene in front of me. The three of them were standing in front of the setting sun when the sunlight made the seawater appear gold in colour. I was still happy with the frame I had in front of me and captured it after seeking the permission of those three people. I showed them the picture of which they asked me a copy. Returning, I overheard a conversation in which the child who was there in the picture called that old man grandpa. I stopped and turned back when the old man was heard calling the other man who first held the hands of the child 'son'. I felt so happy because it is not only that I was able to capture a photograph, but was also able to record a powerful emotion. I looked at the picture once again. A child was being held safely by his father and his grandfather. The image captured a view with one of the strongest emotions in this world – fatherhood.

Next time when you are about to capture an image, think whether the frame also has a story to tell. I clicked the picture on my mobile without caring for its camera settings. You don't always need a good camera. You just need a better frame. And guess what? Great frames are available everywhere. Seek them out.

9
Kind

"Art is when you listen to the universe. Magic is when the universe listens to you."

ᐩᐩᐩ

From the day I started clicking pictures, I liked wildlife photography more than any other genre. Landscape photography is my second favourite genre and creative photography third. Anyhow, as a beginner, I have not got much chance to explore the world with my camera. Going back to Trivandrum zoo where I captured that leopard in a cage, I also got a chance to capture another image which I felt unique. After exploring the section where lions, tigers and leopards were put in, I went ahead to visit peacocks. There was one white peacock which gained everyone's attention. The peacock was inside a cage that had no bars and was covered only with nets. As everyone was admiring the peacock which was standing with its feathers unfurled, I noticed some parrots and wild squirrels playing on a tree near to the peacock cage. Next moment, one wild-squirrel and a parrot saw each other for the first time. They greeted each other with both the animals touching each other's lips.

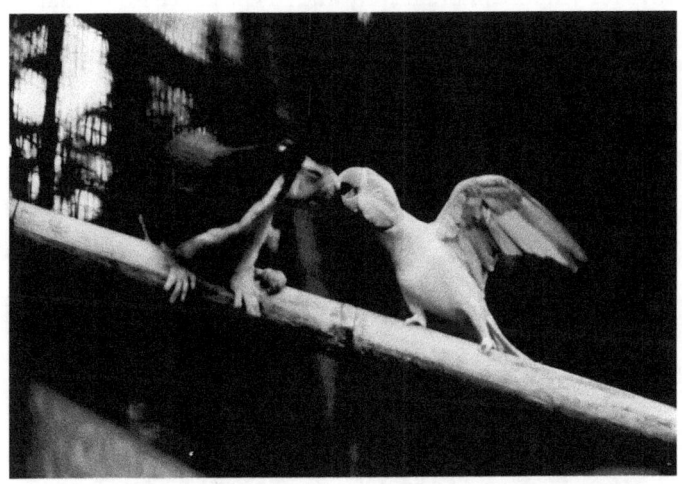

I had never heard of anything like that before. I was thrilled that the photo I took conveyed the emotion of love. It made me realise how much happy and comfortable I was while clicking pictures of animals. A similar instance occurred when I went to Nandi Hills with my friends. Nandi Hills as a tourist destination is always surrounded by monkeys which approach tourists for food and water. I was drinking water from a bottle when a baby monkey came across, asking for it. I thought that the monkey needed some food as it might have misunderstood water to be food. One of my friends handed over a cookie to the monkey while I tried to freeze that moment. I couldn't click a picture while he was handing over the cookie but could click another image with the monkey holding the cookie in his hands. The photograph not only captures a baby animal but also the innocence of a baby. I still believe that I was able to capture the image as it is only because of two reasons – my love for wildlife photography and my patience for the same.

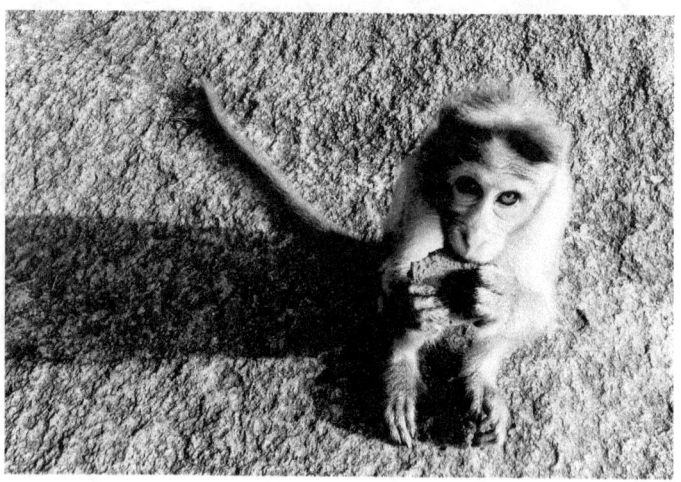

Nowadays, there are different genres of photography. There was a time when the use of tools like lens ball was called as creative photography whereas by now, they are called as lens ball photography. The types and genres of photography are evolving day by day as you may be confused about which genre to specialise in. The first thing you have to consider while selecting a genre for specialisation is why do you want a domain. If you wish to specialise in wildlife photography, think why you want to do so and how much are you comfortable clicking the pictures of wild animals. Same when you choose other genres of photography. You may feel happier when you click photos of landscapes but not so when it comes to shooting animals. You may feel afraid to go into the forests and streets but not to cliffs and mountains. Find which genre suits the best and specialise in it, even if it is a genre specialised by others. In the end, it is better to be unique in a typical genre than to be someone who keeps on seeking unique genres.

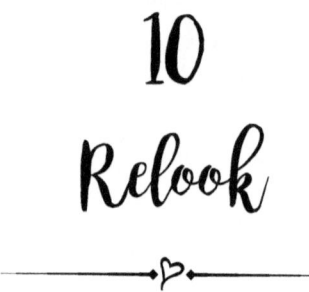

10
Relook

"If you change the way you look at things, the things you look at will change."
- Wayne Dyer

༓༓༓

Elephants are an integral part of the culture of Kerala. You can see them associated with different festivals of the state. One day, as I was standing on a roadside in Thrissur, I saw an elephant being walked by. As a person who loves elephants, I wished to get its picture. The elephant was taken care of by three people, and as they approached, I thought I could capture the animal and its tamers together in one frame.

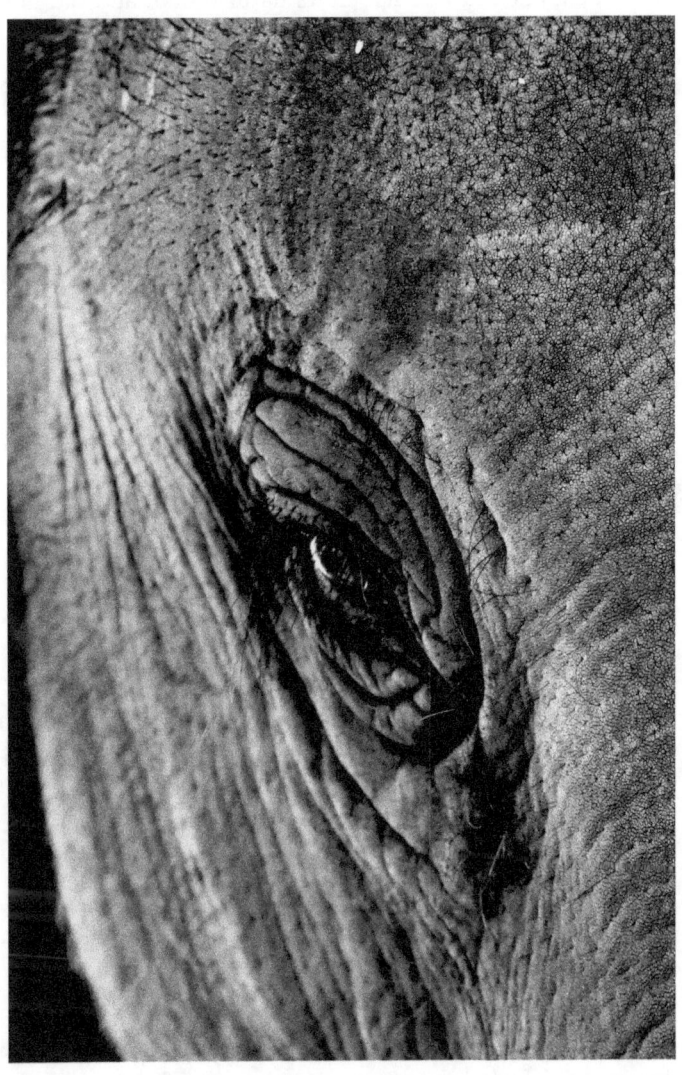

I kept my camera ready with a zoom lens when a thought struck my mind - the elephant is not free. It was tied in chains and was not in its natural habitat. I did not know what to do. I could not resist myself from capturing a photo but did not want to click a picture of an animal in chains. I stood there confused while the elephant came close by. Without thinking much, I held my camera in position and pressed my shutter button. I clicked a picture with the head of the elephant, the centre of focus. The chain with which he was tied was also visible. Coming back home, I relooked the image multiple times, and I wanted to get rid of the chains as much as possible. However, if I remove that chain with a photo editing software, I didn't feel that the image will retain its authenticity. Of course, you can manipulate a photograph as much as you want, making it other forms of art than photography. As a person who wants to capture things as they are, I didn't feel like removing the chains from the elephant. At that time, I noticed the right eye of the animal, which conveyed many emotions and told numerous stories. It reflected power, faith and love hidden behind suffering and separation. Without thinking much, I used the crop tool and sliced the picture in such a way that the elephant's right eye became the photograph's centre of attraction.

Often, doing some basic retouch on a photograph such as adjusting brightness, contrast, and cropping are acceptable in many photography platforms. These platforms may be reputed magazines, photography exhibitions and photography competitions. It is better to adhere to such retouches than manipulating an image using editing software if you wish to retain its authenticity. However, I feel that every artist has the freedom to do whatever they want with their artworks. Manipulated images thus become a new kind of art than photography. Next time when you are confused about whether you should edit your picture or not, it will be better if you understand why you want to edit it in the first place. Is it because you want to retouch and remove unwanted objects from the frame, or is it because you want to make it another kind of art?

Once, Picasso was asked what his paintings meant. He said, "Do you ever know what the birds are singing? You don't. But you listen to them anyway." So, sometimes with art, it is important just to look.

"When it is all finished
You will discover
It was never random."

Acknowledgements

Sometimes I just look up, smile and say, "I know that was you. Thank you." Thank you, God, for making this dream come true. Thanks to my readers for taking your valuable time to check my ideas. My gratitude to Notion press publications for providing opportunities to budding writers like me. Thanks to all the photographers out there for showing me what the art of photography is in your way. I would like to express my gratitude to all those who offered and will offer help, comments and feedback to this book and to the photographs I take.

"Art is never finished, only abandoned."
- Leonardo Da Vinci

www.ingramcontent.com/pod-product-compliance
Lightning Source LLC
Chambersburg PA
CBHW071727170526
45165CB00005B/2187